Bill Milton started his working life on the production line in a factory before joining a Merchant Bank in the City where he spent over 30 years, culminating in him becoming head of the training department in a Swiss Bank. Following his retirement, Milton started to write poetry for friends and family and was persuaded to have a collection of his work published.

Inspired by the poetic works of John Cooper Clarke

Bill Milton

# GIANT FOOTSTEPS

AUSTIN MACAULEY PUBLISHERS™

LONDON • CAMBRIDGE • NEW YORK • SHARJAH

ISBN 9781035819676 (Paperback)
ISBN 9781035819683 (ePub e-book)

www.austinmacauley.com

First Published 2023
Austin Macauley Publishers Ltd®
1 Canada Square
Canary Wharf
London
E14 5AA

A big thanks to wife, Jackie and Gary, Will and Henry for their support and encouragement.

# 1. Giant Footsteps

Mandela's long walk to freedom,
Mahatma Gandhi's peaceful plan.
Neil Armstrong landed on the moon.
Who will take the next step for man?

Charlie Chaplin with his bowler,
Walking cane and shabby suits.
Will there ever be another?
Who will wear the Maestro's boots?

Elvis Presley and John Lennon,
Louis Armstrong with his beat,
Frank Sinatra and Bob Marley.
Who will make us tap our feet?

Eric Morecambe, Ernie Wise,
Tommy Cooper's puzzled face,
Stan and Ollie and Max Miller.
Who will ever take their place?

Ingrid Bergman, Judy Garland,
Betty Davis, Lucille Ball,
Doris Day and Katie Hepburn.
Will any others walk that tall?

Coco the Clown and Grimaldi,
Always managed to amuse,
Famous clowns throughout the ages.
Can anybody fill their shoes?

# 2. Insecticide

The earwig was earwigging.
The flea scratched his head.
The bug overheard
What the spider had said.
The fly was annoyed
That he was not on the wall,
Where he could have listened
And spread gossip to all.

The moth's in a lather
As the truth came to light.
The misinformation
Had reached a new height.
The wasp made a beeline
To question the worm,
Who had the best view
And the facts could confirm.

The spider announced,
What he'd seen on the web.
'Butterfly had been snatched
And presumed to be dead.'
The last time he was seen,
He was caught in a net,
Now he's pinned to a board
Which made the insects upset.

# 3. Imaginary Friends

They laughed when I said my imaginary friend
Was the only pal that I had.
They laughed when I said my imaginary friend
Was one hell of a lad.
They laughed when I said my imaginary friend
Thought me a bit of a schmutz.
They laughed when I said my imaginary friend
Told me he hated my guts.

I laughed when they told me they had many friends
Contacted on Facebook each day.
I laughed when they told me they had many friends
Who loved to read what they say.
I laughed when they told me they had many friends
Like me they can't really see.
I laughed because they have imaginary friends
So why are they laughing at me?

# 4. I Never Forget a Face

The dad of my best friend was forgetful,
He sometimes got lost without trace.
I remember he went missing at Ascot,
On the day Frankel won his last race.

A few years later while shopping in Tesco,
That same gent stood looking confused.
I went over to Charlie to offer some help
But my assistance he roundly refused.

I returned to my trolley very concerned
That I shouldn't leave Charlie alone.
I went back once again to try to explain
Saying I was a friend of his son.

'You know my boy' replied the old man
'Has been working away in Qatar.'
This wasn't true as I'd seen him last night,
So I took my mate's dad to the car.

'Please do up your seatbelt, I'm taking you home,
I'll come in and make you some tea.
There you are Charles, you're home safe and sound,
Let me help you look for your key.'

'Wait by the gate with your bags of shopping
While I give your Gordon a call,
I must admit you look a bit different,
I didn't realise you were tall.'

'Hello Gordon I've rescued your father,
What do you mean he is with you?'
'Who's this old man I've taken to Charlie's,
He has started to shake and turn blue.'

# 5. Already Seen

The term déjà vu
I once heard before.
On what occasion,
I'm not really sure.
The feeling I got
When this phrase was used,
Has stuck in my brain
And left me confused.

The term déjà vu
I once heard before.
On what occasion,
I'm not really sure.
The feeling I got
When this phrase was used,
Has stuck in my brain
And left me confused

# 6. Made in Heaven

A Grandson asked where he had come from.
His Granddad didn't know how to reply.
He stuttered 'God sent you from heaven,
You're our little gift from on high.'

The young boy looked at his Grandpa.
'Did God make you and Granny as well,
'Cos he gave you a face full of wrinkles
And also a very strange smell?'

The boy saw his Granddad's expression.
'Granddad, please don't look so sad,
All those years ago when he made you,
The Lord God was only a lad.'

'Perhaps God didn't have a steam iron.'
Said the old man with a sly grin.
'But now he's had years of practice,
So he presses everyone's skin.'

'The reason I'd asked where I'd come from,
Was the boy who sits next to me,
Announced to the rest of the class,
That he came from Southend-on-Sea.'

# 7. Shell Shocked

Where can my tortoise have gone?
I turned my back for a second or two,
How he escaped I haven't a clue.
Where can my tortoise have gone?

I've searched in the garden,
I've looked in the shed,
I've checked in the garage,
I hope he's not dead.
He might be next door,
Well out of my sight
Eating some lettuce.
I hope he's all right.
Where can my tortoise have gone?

# 8. Nursery Crimes

Animal Cruelty
They may be rodents those three blind mice,
But to cut off their tails was not very nice.

Theft
Piper's son, Tom, committed a crime
For stealing a pig he will have to do time.

Murder
By candlelight a man lost his head,
The killer has left another one dead.

Harassment
Georgy kissed the girls and made them cry,
This nasty bully was cruel and sly.

Discrimination
All girls are made from sugar and spice,
Boys from things that are not at all nice.

Child Cruelty
The Old Shoe Lady her own kids would beat
And send them to bed with nothing to eat.

G.B.H.
Because an old man would not say his prayers,
He was cruelly abused and thrown down the stairs.

Bigamy
A man who was coming home from St Ives,
Openly admitted he had seven wives.

Substance Abuse
It was a spliff in the afternoon,
That made the cow jump over the moon.

# 9. Fair Warning

An old woman wanted a parrot,
She was lonely and lived on her own.
One was being sold at the auction,
She contacted them using the phone.

The guide price was listed as twenty,
The lady bid that very amount,
A voice at the back upped the ante,
As the excitement started to mount.

Her reply was quick and decisive,
She offered to pay forty-four,
Someone at the rear made it fifty,
So the woman put forward ten more.

After a few seconds of silence,
A new figure was heard from behind.
One hundred—the sum was repeated.
Had this 'man' taken leave of his mind?

The next call was to double the price
Which concluded the fight for the lot.
The auctioneer said the bird is yours
And what a fine parrot you've got.

Who was it that forced me to go high
And pay more than I wanted to do?
He must really have yearned for the prize
Just as I had desired it too.

The old lady was in her front room,
Wishing her parrot's talking would stop.
'One hundred—I repeat one hundred.'
At last the penny started to drop!

# 10. Two Types

Harold Macmillan,
But not Tony Blair.
Oliver Hardy,
But not Fred Astaire.
Martin Luther King
And Vincent Price,
Plus Joseph Stalin,
But not Sir Tim Rice.

Neville Chamberlain,
And Buffalo Bill,
Groucho and Chaplin,
But not Benny Hill.
Sir Edward Elgar
And George Bernard Shaw,
Salvador Dali,
But not Roger Moore.

Trevor McDonald,
As well as John Cleese.
Mark Twain and Hulk Hogan
And sometimes Vic Reeves.
William Shakespeare,
But not Ernie Wise.
The Scarlet Pimpernel
When he's in disguise.

Samuel L. Jackson
And Rufus Hound.
Not Winston Churchill
Or Gordon Brown.
Who goes in which group
And why should that be?
Visualise faces
And what do you see?

# 11. Breaking and Entering

Goldilocks what were you thinking
Breaking into somebody's home?
You waited 'til the bears went out,
And stole food that you didn't own.

Why did you ransack their dwelling,
Leaving a chair broken in two?
You left their place in a shambles,
Why you did it we haven't a clue.

You fell asleep on Baby Bear's bed
That is how the police report goes.
They surprised you when they returned
So you had it away on your toes.

Goldilocks you've gone to a place
Where they serve porridge each day.
Baby Bear still suffers from flashbacks
Due to the time you came to stay.

# 12. Rolled

Charlie had an Oxo tin
That he kept his marbles in.
Charlie knew he'd always win
And add more marbles to his tin.

A mugger with a surly grin,
Snatched the treasured Oxo tin.
An old lady with a rolling pin
Sent the felon into a spin.

She kicked the robber in the shin,
Wiping away his evil grin.
A policeman heard the awful din
And ran the battered mugger in.

Prison will be his price for sin
And soon his sentence will begin.
Now Charlie's got his Oxo tin
With his precious marbles in.

# 13. Circle of Life

We used to meet back in the day
And talk about the night before,
Which one of us had drunk the most
And all the latest clothes we wore.
Who did what and who went where
And who went out with who.
The Sixties saw us having fun
As we talked the evening through.

The years have not been kind to us
And on occasions we still meet.
We talk about the pills we take
And the problems with our feet.
We don't speak about the night before
Because we were all tucked up in bed.
We've thrown the things we used to wear
And now we dress for warmth instead.

We used to talk back in the day,
What it would be like to grow old.
We did not believe those grumpy gits
And all the tales that we were told.
Now we're the ones who bellyache
About all the troubles that we've got.
The young talk about the night before,
Who went where and who did what.

# 14. Sit Back and Relax

Put the protective goggles on
And sit right back in the chair.
I want to ask you some questions
About hygiene and dental care.
How often do you brush your teeth
And how many times do you floss?
By the plaque and tartar collected,
I don't believe you give a toss.

You say you use an electric brush,
Surely that really can't be true!
I will show you how to work one
And all the things you have to do.
Please sit still while I check your gums
And get rid of last night's tea.
If the water starts to choke you
Do not spit it over me.

Open wide and turn to the right,
You will not feel too much pain.
I will try not to touch the nerve,
I need to rid you of that stain.
Are you going on holiday this year?
Sorry I can't hear your reply,
Please do not remove that instrument
It will keep your drenched mouth dry.

That wasn't too bad now was it?
Just two X-rays and we are done.
Rinse and get rid of all that blood,
The biggest shock is yet to come.
Stay seated for a few more secs
While I extract your credit card.
The high cost of this procedure
May well leave you dentally scarred.

# 15. Text Addict

Young Bradley Dexter,
A compulsive texter,
Never took his eyes off his phone.
When dining with friends,
He constantly sends,
Replies to all messages shown.

Bradley's wife Alexa,
Hated her texter,
He would not look up at her face.
When walking in town,
He'd mow people down,
Knocking kids all over the place.

Young Bradley Dexter,
Didn't know that Alexa,
Had left him two weeks ago.
He refused to believe
That one day she'd leave
And he'd be the last one to know.

When Bradley Dexter,
Heard from wife, Alexa,
It took time for him to cotton on.
There was only one way
For Brad's spouse to say,
It was by text to tell him she'd gone.

# 16. A Fine Innings

No one understood why
Duckworth loved cricket.
He told us he was once—
Dismissed 'Leg Before Wicket'.
He said he'd got a 'Wrong'un'
Caused by the reverse swing.
This went over our heads
And did not mean a thing.

Duckers spent hours talking
About Sliders and Spin,
Night Watchmen and Bouncers,
Who is out and who's in.
Silly Point and Third Man
The pain when he got struck.
Those Jaffas and Beamers
When he fished for a duck.

His best knock was ninety
Which few Englishmen score.
He played with a straight bat
And stood firm for a draw.
He picked out the googly
And full toss to his head.
Many years in the game
Meant he was not misled.

Duckworth struggled to cope
The years started to show.
His joints began to ache
And reactions were slow.
He ran for a second,
His ground he did not make.
He walked to the clubhouse
For Viagra and cake.

# 17. Get a Man In

Jonah's spouse was frustrated
At all the jobs he had botched.
He loved D.I.Y. programmes,
They were the shows that he watched.

Each task he keenly tackled
'Til his concentration lapsed.
After each job's completion,
The project always collapsed.

He built a bookshelf one Christmas,
It fell down by New Year's Eve.
The weight of books made it tumble
Which his wife could not believe.

After his latest disaster,
He thought he would stick to glue.
A curtain pole needed fixing
Which was on his list of 'To Do'.

In the night there was a loud crash,
The rod fell with curtains and all.
The racket woke up the household,
When the rail detached from the wall.

'Enough is enough' he was told
'Don't enter the house with your tools,
You are confined to the garden.'
He was made to keep these new rules.

Jonah started work on a shed,
Built with his best friend out of wood.
His wife did not know he had help
And was surprised that it still stood.

# 18. Like It or Lump It

At nearly four years of age I was sent
To stay with my Great Aunt Alice in Kent.
A Victorian lady with a stern face,
Most of her frock was adorned with black lace.

'Go and sit right down you miserable boy
And don't play with the cat he's not a toy.
Hand over those sweets that you've just got out,
You'll learn to behave you horrible lout.'

Aunt Alice, of course, had no kids of her own
And apart from her cat lived all alone.
'Boy come for your dinner and eat every bit,
If you leave a morsel your legs will be hit.'

The gravy she made was as cold as her heart
With large sticky lumps that I could not part.
The cabbage was mushy and Brussels were hard
And the potatoes were burnt and covered in lard.

'Put your fork down we have got to say grace,
You really need to be put in your place.
Don't forget eat everything in your dish,
All of the sprouts and not only the fish.'

'You insolent wretch, you've left all your food,
We all know what happens to boys that are rude.
Get under the stairs and sit on the coal,
Reflect nasty child whilst locked in that hole.'

After four hours the door was unlocked,
Auntie Alice stood there looking quite shocked.
Behind the old bat was my angry Dad,
'That is no treatment for any young lad.'

En route through the kitchen I looked about
Nudging the gravy boat as I went out.
There was smashed china and lumps on the floor,
I grinned as I made my way to the door.

# 19. A Knight Came A-Calling

Little Jackie Clarke that was
Lived at number twenty-three.
A knight in shining armour knocked
And I think that man was me.

Little Jackie Clarke that was
Looked like the maiden fair.
'Why are you knocking at my door
And what's with the funny hair?'

Little Jackie Clarke that was
Began to change her mind,
Perhaps that knight is not too bad
If you prefer that kind.

Little Jackie Clarke that was
Soon was Miss Clarke no more,
Perhaps she wished back in the day,
She'd slam the bloody door.

# 20. The Crocodile Rocks

Lizzie the Lizard
Clung on to the wall.
Freddie the Bullfrog
Was having a ball.
The newt got so pissed
He fell out of the lake.
The toad laughed out loud
And so did the snake.
The tortoise was slow
To join in the fun.
The 'gator had slept
Since the party begun.
The chameleon—
Was last seen at eight.
She must have sneaked off
On a prearranged date.
The skink was too drunk
To dance with the gila.
He could not stand up
Had too much tequila.
The eel did the conga
And so did the mamba

The frog did the hop
And the leech did the samba.
The worm did a line dance
As the crocodile rocks.
The reptiles clapped loudly
While the green turtle mocks.
The creatures disbursed
After the last jive.
As they all went home
The snail just arrived.

# 21. Face the Facts

What makes you think I'm on Facebook
And your news will interest me?
I don't want to see your photos
Or be told what you had for tea.
Why would I really want to know
That little Billy's grown an inch?
To be classed as your special friend
Would surely cause me to flinch.

If you have important stuff
That you're unable to postpone
And you feel that it is vital
Then you can reach me on the phone.
It is not a new invention,
They have been using it for years.
You speak into the mouthpiece
And put the headset to your ears.

I have no wish to be on Facebook,
I simply do not have the time.
Wasting all those precious hours
Should be a punishable crime.
You can keep your blessed Facebook
Because I fail to comprehend,
Why the extroverts among you
Need to upstage their only 'friend'.

# 22. Grumpy Old Git

On a very long list of Grandfather's moans,
Are people who can't take their eyes off their phones.
There's Kitty Hognose, who's a silly ol' bat,
Commuters on trains who think it's all right to chat.
Those punk rockers who don't remember 'The Clash'
And councils where you cannot pay using cash.
Selfish parents who park outside of a school,
Wicked means evil, it does not mean cool.
When there's no thanks for holding open a door,
The greedy among us who always want more.
Reality TV that creates so-called 'stars',
All the boy racers who speed in souped-up cars.
Goal celebrations by the footballing rich,
Unable to scratch that inaccessible itch.
Computer instructions that do not make sense,
Politicians who always sit on the fence.
When you have grown old, people think you're not there
And there's only one style they know for your hair.
The afternoon ads that plan when you are dead,
Cyclists that pass through lights that are red.
The conspiracy theorists that freak us all out,
Those well-meaning folk who feel they have to shout.

Motorists who don't signal their intentions,
Anoraks who go to 'Star Wars' conventions.
Youngsters with jeans that do not cover their arse,
Recycling plastic is a bit of a farce.
Traffic congestion, no workmen, just cones,
Snobs that want scons when in fact they mean scones.
Confusing instructions to download an app,
Men who are jobsworths once they put on the cap.
When Granddad passes on and they write his obit,
He wants them to say he was a grumpy old git.

# 23. Bear Baiting

Bruin the Bear was so sad in his pit
Sometimes he would stand, but mostly he'd sit.
Every night he slept on dirty old straw,
Itching his back with the end of his claw.
The public arrived at the start of each day,
They wanted to see the young cub at play.
Bruin pointed his backside at the large crowd,
Releasing some wind that was rancid and loud.

The spectators dispersed as quick as they came
Calling this creature a terrible name.
The grizzly hated the ones that were smug,
If only he could grab one and give him a hug.
He fell asleep before the next group arrived,
'Wake up you old fleabag' a teenager cried.
Bruin turned over and ignored the young lout,
The snub from the bear made the idiot shout.

'Look old fleabag is sneaking back to his den.'
As he turned to the crowd and bellowed again.
Bruin doubled back and hid under the wall,
The thug spun around and started to bawl.
Then he leant forward to find out what was there
Eight feet below him was an angry young bear.
Who let out a roar that would've woken the dead,
The beast mocked the mocker as the young mocker fled.

# 24. Head, Shoulders, Knees and Toes

This morning I've got a sore head.
I'm feeling as if I'm half dead
And will have to stay in my bed.
Last night I was easily led,
There's nothing more to be said
If only I'd used my thick head.

The pain I get in my shoulder,
Gets worse when the weather is colder.
I went to my doctor and told her,
She made a note in her folder.
This happens as we get older
And now I've got the cold shoulder.

As I glance at my swollen knees
They look like I've been stung by bees.
My doc diagnosed Knobbler's disease
After giving my joints a hard squeeze.
Guided by this sound expertise
There's no more getting down on my knees.

There is something wrong with my toes,
The dull ache it comes then it goes.
Why it happens nobody knows,
'Cos they smell much worse than my nose.
It is due to old age I suppose,
Those piggy piss taking toes.

# 25.

# www.punctuationman.comma

I'm the latest superhero,
Punctuation Man is my name.
My costume's made of snake skin
And my logo's an orange flame.

Apostrophe Boy is my sidekick
He will right grammatical wrongs.
By informing the offender
Where the apostrophe belongs.

Questions without question marks,
Semi-colons that are misused,
Quotation marks and hyphens
There is no need to be confused.

We will use our superpowers
And will not fail to do our bit.
When we see bad punctuation,
We will put a stop to it.

# 26. You've Missed a Bit

Fetch me the brushes,
The turps and the rags,
Hand me the dust sheets
Stored in the green bags.
I'll wash the ceiling
And you scrub the walls,
Find a screwdriver—
From my box of tools.

Before we get started,
You can make us both tea,
Fetch some plain biscuits
And Hobnobs for me.
Did you go to the match
And what was the score?
It's time to clock on
Try priming that door.

Pass me your paper,
I'll read for a while.
Remember who's boss
And don't be so vile.
Who taught you the job
And showed you some tricks,
Who always gives you,
A tenth of the tips?

I am off to the shops
To buy some more paint.
Avoid running tears,
We don't want a complaint.
No you cannot stop,
You lazy young git.
I've one thing to say—
You've just missed a bit.

# 27. 'Ello, 'Ello, 'Ello

I took my signed painting to the auction
That was bequeathed to me by my nan.
Gran told me it was by Constable
And therefore must be worth a few grand.

I queued for a quick valuation,
The man said 'ello, what have we here?
This is a high-quality landscape,
But the signature's not very clear.

The expert said he knew the artist
He'd come across his work once before.
This picture was not really worth much
Of that he was reasonably sure.

The oil was by a local policeman,
Who was born in these parts long ago.
He signed all his work Constable John
You can just see his signature below.

The frame is worth more than the canvas
And that'll probably sell for a score.
I'm sorry your hopes have been dashed sir
Which has been the fate of others before.

The art work now hangs in my toilet
And when all my friends go for a pee,
They stand and admire my treasure
And cannot believe what they see.

# 28. The Golden Girl

Herbert has two daughters,
Elizabeth and May.
Mavis went to uni,
But Lizzie went astray.
Mavis got a Desmond
And her sister got expelled
Anything that Mavis did,
The blue-eyed girl excelled.

Herbert had a favourite
Which secretly was May.
He was proud of her achievements,
Although he'd never say.
But when he needed nursing
May was nowhere to be seen
And to Herbert's amazement,
Liz was quickly on the scene.

Herbert phoned his best-loved
To see if she would call.
'Dad I'm very busy'
Oh how the mighty fall.
When the Silver Sister
Went to help her Dad,
She couldn't help but notice
That the old man looked so sad.

Herbert said to Lizzie
I have got things wrong,
Mavis is the weak one
And you're the one that's strong.
In you I see your mother
And your sister is like me.
When I look into the mirror
I'm ashamed at what I see.

# 29. Our Lambeth Slum

We had damp in the basement
And mildew on the wall.
All the floorboards had woodworm
With dry rot in the hall.
But we were 'appy.

There were rats in the kitchen
And dead flies on the meat.
The cockroaches had departed
There was not much to eat.
But we were 'appy.

As we sat on the toilet,
We could see the night sky.
It was cold in the winter
And we hoped it stayed dry.
But we were 'appy.

The house had no electric,
The bath was made of tin,
It was stored in the garden
And each Friday brought in.
But we were 'appy.

Waste scraps went in pig bins,
There was never a lot,
Mostly potato peelings
That is all the swine got.
But they were 'appy

We had rheumatic fever,
German measles and mumps,
Chicken pox and whooping cough
And that illness with lumps.
Why were we 'appy?

# 30. Sick as a Parrot

Baboons need cream for a backside that's sore,
A groundhog will have an off day.
The camel is often down in the mouth,
Donkeys can catch a fever from hay.

Eye drops will not stop a crocodile's tears
And a leopard's spots will never heal.
A woodpecker's headache cannot be eased
Or an otter be helped with his chill.

A coot requires treatment for hair loss
And the newt has a problem with drink.
The skunk has a particular ailment
That causes all its' body to stink.

The aardvark is always first to be called
When it comes to a medical check.
There's no time for anyone else to be seen
If the giraffe has a pain in the neck.

When it comes to taking all his tablets,
The ol' elephant never forgets.
A tomcat is very seldom unwell
Because of his deep-seated hatred of vets.

The one thing that perplexes the doctors
And cuts those physicians to the quick.
Why does a parrot that only eats seed,
Spend his life being constantly sick?

# 31. Doctor Foster's Anatomy

A is for Amnesia—that struck Little Bo Peep.

B is for Bite—that put a princess to sleep.

C is for Cholesterol—Jack Spratt's is so low.

D is for Drugs—which makes Dopey slow.

E is for Earache—that drove Big Ears to pot.

F is for Flu Jab—which Sneezy forgot.

G is for Grief—for Solomon Grundy we weep.

H is for Hypersomnia—the boy in the haystack's asleep.

I is for Injury—when Jill tumbled down.

J is for Jagged Cut—when Jack broke his crown.

K is for Kidneys—that made Wee Willie wee.

L is for Lungs—Wolf didn't blow down house number three.

M is for Musophobia—suffered by the farmer's wife.

N is for Nose Bleeds—that blighted Pinocchio's life.

O is for Obesity—the reason Santa got stuck.

P is for Piles—which made Grumpy suck.

Q is for Queasy—Who was dwarf number eight.

R is for Rickets—the Crooked Man's fate.

S is for Shellshock—that caused Humpty's demise.

T is for Tummy Ache—after Simple Simon ate pies.

U is for Unhealthy Eating—weight Billy Bunter should lose.

V is for Vocal Cords—That Tommy Tucker will use.

W is for Water Retention—When Johnny threw a cat down a well.

X is for X-Ray—used when baby from the tree fell.

Y is for Yellow Fever—not on Captain Pugwash's ship.

Z is for ZZZZ—heard when Sleeping Beauty went to kip.

# 32. Senior Moments

I might be an old fossil—
But I can run up my stairs,
When I get to the landing
I've forgot why I'm there.
I search for the reason,
What the hell could it be.
My brain has gone AWOL
And is no help to me.

I go down to the fridge
And pull open the door.
Why have I gone there
I am not really sure?
I stand in my kitchen,
Trying so hard to think.
I stare into space
As I lean on my sink.

These senior moments
Are a big worry to me.
So I rang up my carer
To ask if he was free.
Come along to my office
And I'll see what I can do.
I said why are you calling
And who the hell are you?

I fetch my medication
That I sometimes get wrong.
I swallow some steroids
Because they make me feel strong.
A tube of Viagra cream
Is applied to my quiff,
It makes my hair hard to comb
As it always goes stiff.

It's no fun growing old,
But still thinking you're young.
Offending the neighbours
With a slip of the tongue.
The G.P. won't see you,
It's a waste of his time,
You can't hear your partner,
So she just has to mime.

The bus pass is a plus,
If I knew where it was.
Forgetting I'd put it
In Auntie Glad's old vase.
So into town I walk
Despite a dodgy knee
The bladder starts to ache
I plan where I can pee.

When I get into Town,
It's a dash for the loo.
This time it's a success
Although not strictly true.
A stranger must be found
To unburden my woes.
Ask their views on Brexit
Which I make sure I oppose.

My short-term memory cells
Started to go on the blink.
I wondered where I was
And found it hard to think.
The next thing I remembered
Was standing in my hall.
I asked the PC with me
Had I been out at all?

# 33. Mustn't Cause a Fuss

The answer to problems
Is a nice cup of tea.
A stare on the tube says,
Why are you looking at me?
Adding salt to your food
Without tasting it first.
Make a dash to the pub
When you've built up a thirst.
If life deals you a blow,
Keep a stiff upper lip.
Insult all your friends
With a readymade quip.
Be quick to say sorry,
Even though you are right.
Never stop to eat lunch,
You just pause for a bite.
Stoke up all arguments
With the opposite view.
Treat people with contempt
Should they not form a queue.
Avoid looking at neighbours
'Cos they might want to talk.

Keep your eyes on the ground
As you go for a walk.
Always use sarcasm
When situations arise.
Save your admiration
For a loser that tries.
On Sunday it's roast beef
Followed by spotted dick.
With lashings of gravy
But it's got to be thick.
To all other nations,
These traits seem quite weird
Our culture is different
That's how we were reared.

# 34. Twist or Bust

A lad from the north of England
Went with his three mates on a cruise.
The ship berthed in Monte Carlo,
The friends slightly worse for the booze.
Les went straight to the casino,
He had not been in one before.
Not being dressed as he should be,
He never got inside the door.

The pals returned a bit later
All four looking ever so cool.
They put their money together,
Giving them a sizeable pool.
The boys showed lots of bravado,
Beginners luck helped them to win.
Collecting two thousand Euros
Because of one fortunate spin.

Very soon they'd spent their winnings
On alcohol and other things.
They went back to the casino
After selling their phones and their rings.
The ship was leaving at midnight,
So on one card they risked the lot.
Lady Luck laughed in their faces
They lost all the cash they had got.

All the way back to Southampton,
Accusations poisoned the air.
The blame was aimed at poor Leslie
Which really was very unfair.
When the lads from the north of England,
Each went their own separate way,
Never forgetting what happened
On that fateful Monaco day.

# 35. A Ten to One Chance

I shone a light on number ten,
Seen standing there were grey-faced men.

I shone a light on number nine,
And saw a lady dressed so fine.

I shone a light on number eight,
Revealing pieces in this state.

I shone a light on number seven
And saw the very best of Heaven.

I shone a light on number six
And spotted half a dozen chicks.

I shone a light on number five,
There stood a bunch reaching up high.

I shone a light on number four,
A fab quartet is what I saw.

I shone a light on number three,
Glimpsing a crowd that don't agree.

I shone a light on number two
A couple sat down for a brew.

I shone a light on number one
There's only me sat in the sun.

# 36. Sleepless in Croydon

You woke me up again last night
By pinching the covers from me.
You gave me one hell of a fright
When you bruised my back with your knee.
As I was about to doze off,
Your mobile phone started to bleep.
The sudden noise led you to cough
Which stopped me from going to sleep.

I tried hard to slumber once more
When an owl decided to hoot.
Meanwhile you continued to snore
Like a tomcat playing the flute.
At last you turned on your side,
Accidentally knocking my face.
I thought I had finally died
And gone to a much quieter place.

# 37. Dear Santa

I have knocked at this house,
'Cos it's last on my list.
I've looked for a chimney,
But one doesn't exist.
Does Jimmy live here?
The boy sent me a note.
He said he's been good
And would like a new boat.

*It has been thirty years*
*Since Jimmy lived here.*
*He waited for a yacht,*
*But one did not appear.*
*Every Christmas Jim wrote*
*To the North Pole address*
*And each year was ignored*
*Which caused him distress.*

The lad's note went astray
And I do not know why.
It's not my intention
To make any child cry.
Do you know where he lives?
I would like to explain
And to say I'm sorry
That I caused him such pain.

*Please don't worry Santa*
*Jimmy did get his yacht.*
*It happened one Christmas,*
*What he longed for he got.*
*He knows you let him down,*
*He's not one of your fans.*
*He saved for his cruiser*
*Which he berths down in Cannes.*

# 38. Give a Dog a Bad Name

We give a dog a bad name
And other creatures too.
But they don't copy humans
And the nasty things we do.

Black cats that cross your path
Are said to bring bad luck.
Not scoring runs in cricket
Is getting out for a duck.

A man is called a chicken
When he gives in to his fears.
Someone making out to weep,
Produces crocodile tears.

A spy or an impostor
Is often labelled a mole.
To call someone a donkey
Will offend a stubborn soul.

A person who talks nonsense
Is said to be spouting bull.
Teenagers who play the goat
Are not considered cool.

Many vindictive females
Are known as bitches or cats.
Treacherous acquaintances
May be described as rats.

A man who tries deceiving
Is called a weasel or a louse.
The question asked of the meek—
'Are you a man or mouse?'

To persistently torment
And the badger gets the blame.
When a person is a loser,
Then we use the turkey's name.

Slippery and devious,
This character's called a snake.
Kangaroo courts are a sham
The justice is always fake.

If a woman is spiteful,
She is likened to a cow.
A man who's very greedy,
He becomes a pig somehow.

So remember when you use
A derogatory term.
These animals have feelings
So don't be a slimy worm.

# 39. Auntie Matilda

I had an Auntie Matilda
Whose hair was as black as the night.
She went along to her wood shed
And received one hell of a fright.
A gnome stood in green pyjamas
With a beard as white as the snow.
He screamed when he saw my Auntie
As she stood with her face all aglow.

The gnome ran into the wood pile,
Matilda made a dash for the door.
Both glanced over their shoulder
And couldn't believe what they saw.
The lady was wearing curlers,
The man had gold shoes on his feet.
My Aunt fell flat on her backside
Which gave her a black and blue seat.

Their fears soon turned into laughter,
The gnome said 'What's that on your face?'
'It's Noxema,' said the old lady,
It keeps all my wrinkles in place.'
The small man glanced down and noticed
He had stained his pyjamas of green.
The old woman went back to her cottage,
She could not believe what she'd seen

Following a disturbed night's sleep,
Matilda was very confused.
Was her recollection a dream,
Brought on by the tablets she'd used?
Auntie returned to the wood shed
To look for some obvious clues.
Perhaps those indentations were—
Footprints made by small pointed shoes.

# 40. It's a Dog-Eat-Dog World

My dog is bigger than your dog,
He is too large for the shed.
He has to sleep in the garage
When he needs to go to his bed.

My dog is fiercer than your dog
With teeth as sharp as a tack.
He'd pounce on him in an instant
And tear the skin from his back.

My dog is loyal not like your dog,
He obeys my every command.
Your mutt ignores all you tell him,
'Cos his dumb and can't understand.

My dog looks better than your dog
With muscles and eyes that are bright.
Your pooch is skinny and nervous,
What good would he be in a fight?

My dog barks louder than your dog,
All your one can do is to whine.
Your house is easy to enter,
But nobody will burgle mine.

My dog has yours stuck in his mouth
Get him out or Tyson will choke.
I did not mean all that I said,
It was just my high-spirited joke.

# 41. Your Call Is Important to Us

This call will be recorded for training purposes
Although we have never trained anyone yet.
If you do not want to queue for a very long time
All information can be found on the Net.
We value our customers and love to hear their views
But we would prefer if you got off the line.
If you're awkward and intend to continue to hold,
Choose one of the options that range up to nine:

Press One if you are a Womble
Press Two if you are called Betty
Press Three if you are a goblin
Press Four if you are The Yeti
Press Five if you are a Muppet
Press Six if you are a big rat
Press Seven if you are a loser
Press Eight if you wear a green hat
Press Nine to hear the menu again,
If you're stupid and think it won't be the same.

The number of time wasters ringing this line is high,
It is time for us to bid you a heartfelt goodbye.
Perhaps next time you will think before you make a fuss,
Remember your call is always important to us.

# 42. The Customer's Always Right

I am sorry you have to wait,
But I am not allowed to serve.
I'd like to see you leave the shop
As you are getting on my nerves.
So what if you are the client,
You'll have to queue like all the rest.
A customer with no manners
Becomes an irritating pest.

Can I talk about my weekend
And the money that I spent?
If you haven't got the patience
Maybe it is time you went.
How do I know they've got your size
And you want me to go and see?
What did your last servant die of
His replacement will not be me?

Stop insisting I go and check
When I am looking for my mate.
I really do not give a toss
If the delay will make you late.
I don't know the manager's name
Or who will handle your complaint.
Whoever has to deal with you
Will need the patience of a saint.

The phone number for Head Office—
I do not have a Scooby-Doo.
I'm not being impertinent
That remark simply is untrue.
I will find someone to help you
Because your stress is so severe.
Then I must go to where I work
Which is certainly not in here.

# 43. Mirror Image

Two old ladies sat in a cafe
Enjoying some tea and a cake,
Boring each other with photos,
The smile on their faces was fake.

Are you coping since your Bert passed
I'm finding it hard without Sid?
I remember his friendly demeanour
And the many things that he did.

Have a look without being seen
At that miserable pair over there.
One has got a face like a turnip,
The other's got greasy brown hair.

When does your Nellie get married
Is it to that man from the pub?
Why have they brought the date forward
Please don't tell me she's in the club?

I'm shocked that you think such a thing,
They said they did not want to wait.
The Council has found them a flat
Which led to them moving the date.

Those two sat at the next table,
I wish they'd drink up and get out.
One likes to do all the talking,
The other's a grumpy old trout.

Perhaps it is time we went home,
I've got washing out on the line.
It is looking as if it might rain,
Yet they said that it would be fine.

I'll go to the foot of our stairs,
Those biddies are about to leave.
One is wearing a coat like yours,
She's even got mud on her sleeve.

They are aping our every move,
I think they are taking the piss.
We all stood up at the same time,
Then I smiled and blew them a kiss.

Don' t look back we are being watched,
Let's beat those old bats to the door.
They seemed to have both disappeared,
We've seen them somewhere before.

# 44. Couplets

How pheasants are bought
And pints in a quart.

Flowerpot men
Twelve minus ten.

Elephant types
Corporal stripes.

Beats in a half note
Sails on a sloop boat.

Number for tea
Five minus three.

Shoes in a pair
Arms on a chair.

The Ronnie's show
Strings to a bow.

Peas in a pod
Ds in 'You're odd'

Number of poles
Halves in a whole.

Beaufort light breeze
And knobbly knees.

Birds on a wall
The yellow ball.

Wings on a bee
Six over three.

# 45. You Can Trust the Fridge

Tomorrow my plane flies to Spain,
Where I will relax and have fun.
Before I leave for the airport,
There are jobs that need to be done.
The curtains will have to be drawn,
The water turned off at the mains.
Several timers must each be set
And the doors secured with chains.

Disconnect the washing machine
And unplug the tumble dryer.
Must not forget the dishwasher,
Or things that might catch on fire.
You can always count on the fridge,
He can constantly be left on.
He's not like the other white goods,
I can trust him when I am gone.

# 46. Teflon Tommy

At Treefell Borough Council,
All complaints will just draw blanks.
The public are a nuisance
And the staff always close ranks.

The head man at the Council,
Never shouldered any blame.
Thomas Tim Macavity,
He was worthy of his name.

His nickname was Teflon Tom
Because nothing ever stuck.
Each time he made an error,
He would quickly pass the buck.

Tom took more in expenses,
Then most people ever got.
What he did for the money
Was quite clearly not a lot.

The Council hates trees and grass
And builds on all green places.
They once built on a sports field
And other open spaces.

The people back in Treefell
Are left with a sprawling mess.
Has Tommy any guilty thoughts
That is anybody's guess?

Due to all the overheads,
Treefell Council has no brass.
There will need to be more charges,
Plus a fee for cutting grass.

A 'Paws Tax' will be brought in
For owning a dog or cat.
A 'High Levy' will be imposed
When a tenant rents a flat.

Youth clubs were axed to raise cash
And here's the comical bit.
The cash was spent on gritters,
But they forgot to purchase grit.

Of course this is all fiction,
No one could be quite that bad.
A comparison to chimpanzees
Would make any monkey mad.

# 47. The Wee Small Hours

There's a structure in my body
That I didn't know was there.
I had no idea what it did
Completely unaware.
This organ is called the prostate,
And keeps me up at night.
My doctor said it's got too big
Which is an old man's plight.

There are a lot of other men
With the same complaint as me.
Who need to ration what they drink
To regulate their pee.
How we all laughed at Grandad
When he was taken short.
We were never sympathetic,
I don't know what he thought.

All the years have floated away,
Light trousers are a no.
There is very little warning
When it is time to go.
Every journey must be planned,
Pinpointing all the loos.
The question that I ask myself—
Which transport do I choose?

# 48. What's in Ivy's Bag

A mobile phone
Her lucky stone
Sherbet suckers
Eyebrow pluckers
Box of matches
Nicotine patches
Two Argos pens
Fisherman's Friends
Various files
Cream for her piles
Packet of pads
Pipe that was Dad's
Balm for her lips
Four paper clips
Syrup of figs
Packet of cigs
Spare pair of knickers
Half-eaten Snickers
Lavender bag
Dirty old rag
Comb and a brush
Something for thrush

Her hair remover
And face improver
Wintergreen rub
Spoons from the pub
A winkle pin
Bottle of gin
Spare set of teeth
Black patch for grief
A powder puff
Some other stuff
Ivy's friend thinks
Who buys the drinks
She starts to curse
There is no purse

# 49. You'll Get No Promotion

Bruce didn't get his promotion again
Because of his immediate boss.
Who laughed when he went to complain
And remarked why should he give a toss.

Bruce went to see his buddy in sales
Who took him to the pub for a drink.
Since he joined, they'd become best of pals
And he wondered what Henry would think.

Henry listen with patience to Bruce
While he supped at his lager and lime.
They decided to have one more juice
As they needed a little more time.

It was during the very next day,
Bruce was offered a job in H.R.
The position attracted more pay
And came with a company car.

His first task was to get rid of staff,
Choosing the people that had to go.
The firm's new henchman stifled a laugh
As his excitement started to show.

The top of the redundancy list
Was the man who was Brucie's old boss.
Who was angry and made a clenched fist
And was told why should I give a toss.

# 50. Sleepover

Mum, I have brought you the Grandkids,
And there's a note in the bag from Kate.
They have both had a few late nights,
So they must be asleep by half eight.
Please don't give them any more sweets,
They've had quite a lot through the day.
Don't give them coke, give them water,
Make sure they don't get their own way.

*We will both follow the orders*
*That have been laid down by your Kate.*
*Do her parents follow these rules,*
*We have heard the kids stay up late?*
*They give them lots of chocolate*
*And sugary drinks before bed,*
*Which is never before midnight*
*At least that is what the kids said.*

They're not allowed on their tablets
Or spend time on the phone after tea.
Teeth must be cleaned after eating,
If they don't report them to me.
They must be up by half seven
For breakfast give them muesli and juice.
Don't let them speak with their mouth full
And don't listen to any excuse.

*Right boys your father has gone home*
*Who wants some cream biscuits and coke?*
*What goes on at Granny's stays here*
*That'll always be our little joke.*
*Tomorrow we'll have bacon and eggs,*
*Followed by strong coffee or tea.*
*If you're ask when you went to bed,*
*Tell them it was eight twenty-three.*

# 51. The Ghost of Joshua Priestly

The ghost of Joshua Priestly
Haunts the alleys of Fogwell-On-Sea.
He was stabbed to death by his wife,
When the two of them couldn't agree.

When the waves crash onto the rocks,
The gullible will hear the loud moans.
Streets close by will turn icy cold
And the fear will penetrate bones.

So if you go to Fogwell-On-Sea
And you hear a heart-rending sound.
You can bet it's Joshua Priestly
As his corpse comes out of the ground.

The apparition will slowly pass,
The spectre of Priestly will fade.
The last thing that's seen is the wound,
Where his spouse plunged in the blade.

If you are one of the sceptics
Spend a night in Fogwell-On-Sea.
Wait until after the pubs shut
When Joshua's spirit roams free.

Now you're a Joshua witness
And can tell all the folks that you meet,
That your blood curdled in Fogwell
From the head right down to the feet.

# 52. No Likes

No, I'm not on bloody Twitter,
You can keep your boring news.
Your comments don't interest me
Or any of your views.

No, I'm not on bloody Twitter
I've better things to do.
I don't want to hear opinions
From people with no clue.

No, I'm not on bloody Twitter,
My thoughts I will not share.
I have no social media friends,
Hashtag, I do not care.

No, I'm not on bloody Twitter,
I don't know how to tweet.
I'll leave that to our feathered friends,
With them we can't compete.

No, I'm not on bloody Twitter,
I wouldn't waste my life.
If I need to hear some tweeting,
I will listen to my wife.

# 53. Nitty Nora

In the early Nineteen Fifties,
The nit nurse ruled the schools.
A metal comb and wooden stick
Were among her many tools.
Each of the head scratching children
Hoped they'd be free of lice.
The dreaded letter sent to Mum
Was never very nice.

Nora called her comb the bug rake
The wooden stick the tease.
Tweezers were known as the grippers
To grab hold of the fleas
The treatment room reeked of Dettol
Also the smell of fags.
The debris from the pupils' scalps
Was safely sealed in bags.

Once the instruments had been cleaned
And the last child had gone.
The Garibaldi's were opened
And the kettle was put on.
Nitty Nora started scratching,
Completely unaware,
That many of the parasites
Had nestled in her hair.

# 54. Bloody Awkward

If you hoot me
I will slow down
Tell me to smile
And I will frown.
When told to think
I blank my mind
Follow the rules
I'm not that kind.
Go with the crowd
I walk alone
You laugh out loud
I like to moan.
My friend and I
Said the right way
Me and my friend
That's what I say.
When shouted at
To step aside
I'll stand my ground
And not move wide.
Don't stroke the dog
'Cos he might bite

He bit my hand
I thought he might.
What do I think
About this or that?
Do you believe
I want to chat?
I will not dance
Do not ask me
Or I'll be rude
As you will see.
Tell me I'm wrong,
I'll state I'm right.
You think It's black,
I'll say it's white.
If you're against,
Then I am for.
I'll disagree,
You can be sure.

# 55. A Bad Hair Day

Poor Katie missed the bus again
When Jane rang her on the phone.
She had to walk home in the rain
And got chilled down to the bone.

Her makeup ran all down her face,
The downpour soaked to the skin.
Kate's hair had all come out of place
And was sticking to her chin.

She couldn't go to the dance that night
Because her hair looked a mess.
Kate thought Jane did this out of spite
Just to put her under stress.

Jane's wicked plan had worked a treat,
Her timing was 'spotty dog'.
She watched Kate from across the street
Making sure she was incog.

The reason for this nasty trick
Was to keep young Kate at home,
Because Jane also fancied Mick
And wanted him all alone.

Fate decided to intervene
When Mick saw Kate was all wet.
He offered a lift in his car
As she appeared quite upset.

Mick and Kate didn't go to the ball,
Instead they went for a meal.
Jane was left to prop up the wall,
Her night had lost its' appeal.

# 56. Selective Hearing

My name is Doctor Shoutloudly,
I'm testing your hearing today.
Your wife arranged for this meeting
And says you won't hear what we say.
The nurse will give you some headphones
And take you to booth number three.
Buzz the buzzer when you are ready
And make sure you are looking at me.

The check went on for twelve minutes
And the patient heard every bleep.
He told the nurse it was easy,
He could do the test in his sleep.
'Why does your wife think you are deaf,
Making this appointment for you.
She said it's not worth her talking
As what she says you haven't a clue?'

# 57. Pounds, Shillings and Pence

Two shillings equalled a florin
And ten florins once made a pound.
Four farthings totalled a penny,
Before decimals were around.
Two and six was half a dollar
And a shilling was named a bob.
A bob was worth twelve old pennies
To lose one would cause you to sob.
A sixpence was called a tanner,
Five shillings was known as a crown.
Four half pennies came to tuppence
An old penny was called a brown.
Twenty-one shillings was a guinea
Or a hundred and five new pence,
Two fifty-two in old money.
Does any of this make much sense?
A ten-shilling note was half a bar
That became the new fifty p.
The symbol for an old penny
Was from denarius, a very small d.
Now it becomes complicated

And you will need all of your wits
To calculate the value of
Eight 12-sided thrupenny bits.
Five three pennies was one and three,
One hundred shillings came to a fiver.
Five pounds was twelve hundred pence,
Known as a Lady Godiva.
The old can work out this money
With no machine to calculate,
All they need is pen and paper
And you won't even have to wait.
When Grandad can't work the computer
Or Granny can't text on her phone.
Could you work out this old money
No matter how often you're shown?

# 58. Why All the Questions?

Why is abbreviated
Such a long word?
Which word is hardest to read
Could it be blurred?
Why is the word gullible
No longer used?
Do you think you're bewildered
Or are you confused?
Two negatives make a positive
That ain't no lie.
Which silkworm won the race or
Did it end in a tie?
Why is the word palindrome
Not one at all?
Should we love a little
Than not a tall?
What's a rhetorical question
How would I know?
I was offered a refuse bin
Why did I say no?
Why does the word alphabet
Have just eight letters

What is a spoonerism—
Lapping first swetters?
Should we have alliterations
Make mine a must?
Why did I sell my Hoover
It was gathering dust?
What are malapropisms
And do they exit?
Is dyslexia a word
I just can't see it?
I learnt twenty-five letters
I don't know why.
Atoms make up everything
Is that why they lie?

# 59. The Seven Deadly Sins

*Lust*

Roger the rabbit had lots of kids,
He could not resist chasing a doe.
On Father's Day he got many cards
As his family continues to grow.

*Gluttony*

Percy the pig was full to the brim,
But did not take his snout from the trough.
His stomach got bigger and bigger
While Percy continued to scoff.

*Greed*

Horace the human took what he could,
Whatever he had just wasn't enough.
He stockpiled his goods and wanted more,
If he was short, he thought life was tough.

*Sloth*

Sammy the sloth spends most of his life
Hanging upside down in a tree.
This mammal sleeps most of the day
Too lazy to find his own tea.

*Wrath*

Grizzly the bear was in a bad mood
Just like a man who had a sore head.
He stayed angry until it was night
And his mother tucked him in bed

*Envy*

All of the hounds were jealous of Blue
Because he was top dog in the pack.
He could jump high, run fast and look good
While the rest stabbed ol' Blue in the back.

*Pride*

Peter the peacock strutted about
Showing his feathers, fanning his tail.
Other birds praised his dancing display,
A fox crept up, Pete's not preening now.

# 60. Rabbit in a Secret Language

Cockney Chas caught the Oxo cube
To go and watch a Shakespeare play.
He took some bread to buy a Rube
At a Gadhafi on the way.
He thought he'd made a Cadbury's flake
'Cos he'd forgot his Peckham Rye.
What if his ticket was Sexton Blake
Which almost made him shirt and tie.
Charlie had got it all Pete Tong
And all was well that ended well.
He found Hamlet a bit too long
In Denmark's flowery dell.
Why was the English that Shakespeare penned
So bleeding hard to comprehend?

# 61. It's Not What You Know

I went to a party
With one of my mates.
We hadn't realised it was posh.
Monogrammed napkins
And bone china plates,
It was clear that someone had dosh.

'Has sir got a drink,
Champagne or Pimm's?'
Said a waiter attired in black.
The glasses were crystal
With pure gold rims,
Beluga was served for a snack.

'Do you work in the City?'
Said a toffee-nosed git.
Who traded in bellies of pork.
'I'm employed by the Duchy,
Where I do not really fit
Because of the way that I talk.'

'You can tell from my accent
I'm not from the South
And I am not one of your nobs.
I wasn't born with the proverbial
Silver spoon in my mouth
Like one of you upper class snobs.'

'I'll go get my coat
And be on my way,
Give my love to Lady Jane Lee.
I am sorry I missed her
On this very strange day,
I will see her this Sunday for tea.'

# 62. Silence Is Golden

Mister Lindley was a teacher of maths
At a school in the county of Berkshire.
He did service in the Second World War
And was captured while fighting in Burma.
When questioned he never said a word.

On demob he went back to his teaching
Where some of the pupils played him about.
Each time his class became loud and unruly,
He just waited not intending to shout.
Deep in thought and without saying a word.

Mister Lindley's hand was broken and gnarled
Which became the subject of many a tease.
But the lack of the slightest reaction
Disappointed any carefully planned wheeze.
The master smiled without saying a word.

One day he had to go to the doctor
And the headmaster took over his form.
He described how their teacher was captured,
Despite torture he refused to inform.
The kids were told that he didn't say a word.

From a shocked and stunned group of students,
The story of courage spread through the school.
His class got to their feet and all cheered
As Mister Lindley sat down on his stool.
Their maths teacher did not utter a word.

As the lesson continued in silence,
One lad asked would he tell some of his tales.
'Please Sir, how did you lose all your fingers?'
Sir replied that he once bit his nails.
The boy sat down without saying a word.

# 63. See No Evil

Who put Monkey down the toilet
And tried to flush him away?
His fur was threadbare and sodden,
His coat bedraggled and grey.

When did they go to my cupboard
To convince Monkey to flee?
Perhaps they doped his banana
And said they'd take him to me.

How did they know where to find him
And that he'd be on his own?
This primate couldn't speak any English,
So he wouldn't have answered the phone.

What was the point of their action
And what did they hope to gain?
Parting me from my Monkey
Caused much emotional pain.

Where did they keep my poor Monkey
While waiting for his cruel fate?
No one should end down a karzee
And left in a terrible state.

Why did they ridicule Monkey,
He nearly went round the bend?
I still have nightmares about it
And how they tortured my friend.

# 64. Say Cheese

Can you name the cheese from the clues
Vincent's the first, he's got the blues?

The next cheese is captured in verse
Because it is made in reverse.

The third one comes in blue and white
Take a sip of port with each bite.

Diner's word, this is a great cheese
From a Royal town if you please.

This one will leave Cat with a grin
'The Best Cheese' is one he might win.

Served on Delilah Hippa's plate
It's found in a very soft state.

Now we reach cheese number seven,
This chess piece smells to high heaven.

The next you can gorge as you wish,
Ideal for a Welsh Rarebit dish.

The ninth is the richest so far,
A creature and old Chelsea star.

A member inside a cat club
Will bring this French cheese for his grub.

Backed by Alan and Jenny Gray
With nettle wrapped back in the day.

Finally, 'The Queen' of the lot
When eaten with Bier hits the spot.

# 65. A Second Opinion

My neighbour's a bit of a smart arse,
He can always tell why I am sick.
A good friend of his had the same look
And this pal's end came painfully quick.
My eyes told him my liver was shot,
I should enjoy my life while I can.
It was his considered opinion
That I was an extremely ill man.
He thought I must be somewhat depressed,
Now that my health was going all wrong
I replied I was feeling quite well
'Til some prophet of doom came along.
Yes, I know what you mean he replied
We have quite a few where I work.
When I try to correct what they say,
I am called a pompous old jerk.
My opinion is usually right
Because I've learnt a lot from the Net
That's how I know you're not feeling good,
But there is no point getting upset.

Mister Know-It-All soon disappeared,
I hope his diagnosis was wrong.
I don't always believe what he says,
He has not been my doctor for long.

# 66. Is It Something I Ate?

Last night I slept very heavy
They were drilling for coal in my head.
I went to the pub for a bevy,
But drank whisky and gingers instead.

When I woke my Mum stood there grinning,
She offered me some bacon to eat.
The room was continually spinning
And I threw up all over her feet.

She shouted for spoiling her slippers,
It must have been something I ate,
Most probably yesterday's kippers
That led me to be in this state.

I've got the shakes and my mouth is dry
And I keep going along to the loo.
I feel as if I'm going to die,
It's strange what herrings can do.

Just in case this was caused by the drink,
It's the hair of the dog that I need.
Something had taken me to the brink
Was this due to a gluttonous greed?

I will never touch whisky again,
This time I will be true to my word.
There's a jackhammer pounding my brain
And my eyes are throbbing and blurred.

# 67. Chain of Command

The General told the Brigadier,
'Get everybody ready to drill.'
The Brigadier informed the Colonel,
'All the squaddies are going to Deal.'
The Colonel instructed the Major,
'Fall the men in we're marching to Rhyl.'
The Major advised the Captain,
'Call to affirm the orders are real.'
The Captain asked the Lieutenant,
'Haul the infirm to the top of the hill.'
The Lieutenant surprised the Sergeant,
'Tell the soldiers to sit down and chill.'
The Sergeant barked at the Corporal
'Yell at those unfit clowns to sit still.'
The Corporal shouted at his troops,
'Get everybody ready to drill.'

# 68. Mistaken Identity

Sitting on the beach down in Worthing
When the storm clouds gathered above.
I rushed to the Connaught Theatre
To see another show I might love.

A man stood alone in the foyer,
He said 'The show is about to begin.'
So I quickly paid for a ticket
And then I was allowed to go in.

Sitting at the front of the stalls,
The anticipation started to grow.
The applause built to a crescendo
I tried to spot the star of the show.

'Mister Hamilton in the right gear,
A role model of the new age.'
When the curtains started to part,
It was Andy who stood on the stage.

# 69. En Garde

The pen is mightier than the sword
Announced Professor Smug Git the Third.
It's easy to defeat all your foes,
With the power of the written word.

The sword became no match for the pen
When the professor wrote to 'The Times'.
The courts are too soft on offenders
And the sentences don't fit their crimes.

After a lecture he loaded his Rolls
Following a week of working away.
The boot was filled with valuable things
That should not have been left on display.

Nick Hall had a history of theft,
He knocked Smug Git the Third to the ground.
Taking all his treasured possessions
Before the posh intellectual came around.

The poor victim had one big regret
That his only weapon was his pen.
The outcome would have been different,
If he could do it all over again.

Unbeknown to ol' Smug Git the Third
The felon's scheme did not go to plan.
A witness managed to find a pen
And took down details of Minster Hall's van.

# 70. They Used to Make Us Chuckle

Eric Morecambe, Ernie Wise
At the top is no surprise.
Naughton, Nervo, Knox and Gold,
The Crazy Gang from days of old.
Brian Rix and Noel Coward,
Joyce Grenfell, Frankie Howerd.
Tommy Cooper, 'Just like that'
Lou Costello's crazy hat.
George Robey, P.M. of Mirth
Harry Secombe, Harry Worth.
Deryck Guyler, Sykes and Hattie,
Kathy Staff as Nora Batty.
Spike Milligan, Peter Sellars,
Two extremely funny fellas.
Jerry Lewis, Lucille Ball,
Norman Wisdom and Max Wall.
Arthur Askey and Ted Ray
Made us laugh back in the day.
Charlie Chester, Clement Freud,
Buster Keaton, Harold Lloyd.
June Whitfield with Terry Scott

Should not ever be forgot.
Arthur Lowe with Clive Dunn
All those soldiers having fun.
Beryl Reid and Beatrice Lillie,
Marie Lloyd and Vesta Tilley.
Peter Cook and Dudley Moore,
Leslie Nielsen, Sammy Shore.
Ronnie B and Ronnie C,
Stanley Baxter, Dustin Gee.
Roy Hudd and Phyllis Diller,
Benny Hill and Max Miller.
Stan and Ollie, what a mess
Hinge and Bracket, in a dress.
Larry Grayson 'Shut That Door'
With the glasses that he wore.
Court Jester, Roland Farter
Bob Monkhouse and Jack Carter.
Eddie Large and Bobby Ball
With their partners they were cool.
Stanley Unwin's clever talk,
Charlie Chaplin's funny walk.
Little Tich, Coco the Clown,
Alan Carney, Wally Brown.
Groucho Marx and his brothers
And many, many, many others.

# 71. Who's Kidding Who?

I've reached the age of eighty-two
And I voted to remain.
My favourite film is Akachu,
Each day I like to game.
My Grandchildren say I am weird
Which I think is unfair.
They do not like my long grey beard
Or salt and pepper hair.
They're mystified by what I know
And surprised by what I don't.
They're astonished by where I go
And amazed by where I won't.
When I add up sums in my head,
They look at me in awe.
I'm sure they feel they've been misled,
But really can't be sure.
When they hear a favourite song
Their faces turn to shock.
As word perfect I sing along,
Winding back the clock.
When I've a problem with my phone
That I don't understand.

I have to listen to them moan
before they lend a hand.
'Press this button and then that one,
Download the latest App.
We're jealous of your Apple phone,
You are a lucky chap.'
They won't swear in front of Granddad,
But little do they know,
This fossil once was Jack the Lad
Which was many moons ago.
Next birthday I am eighty-three,
I'm going on a cruise.
I will take one Grandkid with me,
But which one will I choose?

# 72. Piggy's Pigout

Young 'Piggy' Hogg has eaten too much again,
Despite all the warnings he could not abstain.
The belt round his middle broke under the strain,
Now this human dustbin is bent up in pain.

Starting with bread and a selection of meats,
He then finished off a large packet of sweets.
This was followed by several dishes of treats,
Nothing is wasted when young 'Piggy' Hogg eats.

The food on display was a feast for the eyes,
'Piggy' got stuck in to a plate of mince pies.
Soon he swiftly moved on to burgers and fries,
Mixing so many foods was not at all wise.

He noticed a table with hot dogs and mustard,
Next to a table where others were clustered,
Helping themselves to sponge pudding and custard,
Unable to have both he become flustered.

He could not resist chunky chips with his steak
And two scoops of ice cream complete with a flake.
He also found room for rich chocolate cake,
But could not make out why his belly did ache.

# 73. Anyone for Tennis

Each Wednesday we meet at court number three,
Thomas, Richard, Harold and me.
Harry brings thick glasses so he can see,
Tom a support for his bad knee.
Richard and Thomas can never agree
Then one of them goes for a pee.
Today we're joined by a man called Jack Lee
Thomas, Richard, Harry and me.

Richard goes early because of his back
Leaving Tom, H, me and young Jack.
Tom missed his shot and gave Harry a whack
We all heard a terrible crack.
Harold sank like the proverbial sack,
His leg was bent and slowly turned black
Tom turned green and started to yak.
Closely followed by me and young Jack.

Thomas went with Harry in Harry's car
To A and E which wasn't too far.
Jack said to me it has all been bizarre,
Let's pack up and go for a jar.
I said out loud give that man a cigar
As me and Jack Lee went to the bar.
The events of the day left a bad scar,
Four old fossils and one young star.

# 74. Who Is Banksy?

Jack Nicklaus is the Golden Bear,
Anne of Cleeves was the Flanders Mare,
Harry Crosby was known as Bing,
Elvis Presley was called the King.
William Ralph was Dixie Dean,
Elizabeth One, The Virgin Queen,
Sir Ken Dodd was nicknamed Doddy,
Neville Holder's known as Noddy.

Duke was the nickname of John Wayne,
Martha Canary, Calamity Jane.
Nathaniel Coles was Nat King Cole,
Aretha Franklin, Queen of Soul.
John Kennedy was J.F.K.
Billie Holiday, Lady Day.
Joe Frazier was Smokin' Joe
Maureen Connolly, Little Mo.

Dwayne Henry Johnson is The Rock,
John Holliday was known as Doc.
The Cheekie Chappie was Max Miller
And Jerry Lee was called The Killer.
Donatien, The Marquis de Sade,
William Shakespeare was The Bard.
Boris Karloff was born Will. Pratt
And Philip Tufnell is The Cat.

Mary Mallon was Typhoid Mary,
Melanie Brown is known as Scary.
Terence Milligan was called Spike,
Eisenhower was known as Ike.
Benny Goodman was King of Swing
And Gordon Sumner was named Sting.
Banksy will go down in history,
Who he is remains a mystery.

# 75. Theerz Nowt S' Queer as Folk

Hargreeves went down the ginnel reet quick
He'd gone for a sneck lifter at t'pub.
His lass had monk on before he left
She was narky as they had no grub.

Hargreeves returned yarn ruddy nithered
Having brought nowt to eat for their tea.
His wife shouted that he was a wasak
And he said 'Don't keep mithering me.'

Hargreeves' wife was radged and wanged watter
Which gave him summat to make him roar.
He was flummoxed why she had soaked him,
Why she had, he was not really sure.

Hargreeves knew he had to get some scran,
He would be locked out while he bought food.
So he trotted off to the garage,
There were nowt so he knew he was screwed.

He sat on corser edge so he could think,
How could he tell his lass he'd got nowt.
He would have to man-up and confess
And he reckoned he knew she would shout.

He caught her chelpin' to their neighbour
And got invited in for a mash.
He could smell the havercakes in t'oven
And on the stove some leftover hash.

Hargreeves was a little bit ocker,
He didn't know if his lass would be reight.
'Appen he were out of the dog house,
Mebee that would be an end to the fight.

# 76. Factory Fodder

Clang, Clang, Clackety, Clackety, Clack.
The foreman bellowed label or cap?
Bang, Bang, Taperty, Taperty, Tap.
What an induction for any new chap.
Speed up the line, the bonus is fine,
A penny a thousand if you're on time.
The machines thunder to the beat of a rhyme,
The noise is so loud, the workers must mime.
Clump, Clump, Clumpety, Clumpety, Clump.
Four thousand to go all hands to the pump.
Crash, Crash, Screechity, Screechity, Strump.
How high you must say when you're told to jump?
Heads start to thud as the decibels rise
And the chemical fumes irritate eyes,
But meeting the target is the number one prize,
As the workers' welfare no longer applies.
The pounding machines slow down the clock.
Knock. Knock, Knockety, Knockety, Knock.
The face on the timepiece is starting to mock.
Tick, Tick, Tickety, Tickety, Tock.
Cans have exploded at the start of the belt,
In the next room the shock waves are felt.

The plastic screens have all started to melt,
Those that can be spared must hurry to help.
Waaaahhh, Waaaahhh, Nee Na, Nee Na, Wee.
The siren is sounding, all stop for some tea,
There's a twelve-minute break for a drink and a pee,
Production will resume at ten twenty-three.
The silence is broken by Bang, Whackety, Whack.
The supervisors count everyone back,
Anyone missing will be given the sack
Return to your zone while avoiding the flack.

# 77. The Cat's Whiskers

Peter the Cheetah,
The fastest of cats.
A mile in a minute
Is just one of his stats.

Peter the Cheetah,
Liked having fun,
Showing the gazelles
How fast he could run.

He sits with a mirror,
Perched high in the trees.
Perfection he sighed
He likes what he sees.

Peter thought he looked good
With his shiny black spots.
The ladies adored him,
He guessed there were lots.

A couple of females
Both dated Peter,
Not knowing he was
A two-timing cheetah.

# 78. Plans of Wives and Men

The house met Pat and Pete's expectations
Over an acre of land with the sale.
Spare bedrooms for visiting relations,
Their offer for this place must not fail.
With a cellar, a hot tub and a pool,
In a position where neighbours can't pry.
A double garage and close to a school
Made the couple very eager to buy.
Both were delighted with the location,
The coast was less than seven miles away,
With a five-minute walk to the station
And country parks where the children can play.
The property offered them perfection
That evening would be a time for reflection.

That night Pete was the first to start dreaming
About how he'd like their new home to look.
So he started contemplating and scheming,
He would plan every cranny and nook.
The indoor pool he'd use after training,
The cellar he could turn into a gym.
After lifting weights with all of the straining,

He could cool down in the pool with a swim.
He could replace the lawn with a games court
And construct a pub bar in the shed.
The T.V. could be used to watch all sport,
All those thoughts went around in Pete's head.
He couldn't wait to put his proposals to Pat
As all will be revealed when they both chat

While her husband was dreaming so was Pat
Of using the shed for her exercises.
She would grow roses and keep the lawn flat
In the hope she would win gardening prizes.
The swimming pool she would have removed
The space would be used for her arts and crafts.
The dining room and lounge would be improved
Where her visitors would have tea and laughs.
The cellar would be painted to look bright,
A place where the children can go to play.
It will be used as Pete's office at night
And this will keep him well out of the way.
She looked forward to telling her Hun,
The great many things that need to be done.

# 79. Uncle Ted's Attic

Sadly, Uncle Ted passed away,
He would have been age ninety-three.
The family laughed when I told them,
He'd left his possessions to me.

The Council wrote on the Friday
Without any feeling at all.
'Remove all of Mister Brown's rubbish,
This Monday we will come and call.'

The weekend was spent sorting through,
A lifetime of memories and dreams.
I tried to keep all that I could,
There was far too much so it seems.

The first in the van went his cones
And then his collection of pipes.
In a basket under the sink
Were socks over twenty-two types.

In a cardboard box in a drawer
Was Teddy's Military Cross.
There was an album of photos
Of all the loved ones he'd lost.

That day was spent packing stuff up
As I worked late into the night.
I knew soon the Council would call
'Cos the time was getting real tight.

I just had the attic to clear
Which did not take me too long.
I could not see much through the tears,
Knowing how they'd got Ted all wrong.

The last thing was a case in my name
Addressed to 'my best friend and heir'.
All the sovereigns that it contained,
Ted had made me a millionaire.

# 80. Under Starters Orders

The horses are off with 'Third Place' in the lead,
Chased by 'Failure' in his attempt to succeed.
Then there's a big gap to the horse 'Platform's Edge',
'Cropper' has fallen at the very first hedge.
The last jockey to jump was on 'Runner-up',
Who the previous year had won the Gold Cup.

'Winner' and 'Daddy's Yacht' sailed over the fence,
The Owners looking on were ever so tense.
'Drop Down to the Ground' unseated his rider,
Priced twenty to one he was the outsider.
At the next hurdle all the runners jumped clear
'Tight Jeans' faded away and brought up the rear.

'Daddy's Yacht' appeared to have sank without trace,
But 'Failure' was running an excellent race.
'Tight Jeans' fell down at the penultimate jump
And 'Platform's Edge' took a terrible thump.
'Best-Loved', the favourite, pulled up at the last
The grey mount, 'Runner-up' went thundering passed.

The four nags in contention dashed for the post,
It was a question of who wanted it most.
'Third Place' was the winner, 'The Winner' came third,
'Failure' took second after he had been spurred.
'Runner-up' came in fourth just outside a place
No others finished The Perplexity Chase.

# 81. Why the Long Face?

Yes Son, you can have a pet.
Great Mum, I will have an 'orse.
Where do you think you'll keep it?
Why Mum, in a field of course.
But Son, we live in Brixton
Where there is hardly any grass,
When you lead it down the street,
They'll say there goes an 'orse's arse.

# 82. You Can Take It with You

An old man suspected that his end was near,
So he thought it was time to chat with his wife.
'I want you to promise me that when I die,
You'll put my cash in with me for the next life.'

The old lady swore she would honour his wish
And gathered all the fivers from under the bed.
She put them somewhere safe until the time came,
Sadly, within days her dear husband was dead.

After the service she sought out her best friend
And told her the oath she had made to her bloke.
'Don't tell me you put all that cash in the box
And now all that money has gone up in smoke.'

She told her friend exactly what she had done
Keeping the promise she had made to her spouse.
A cheque had been placed in the casket with him
While the wad of notes was kept back at the house.

To her surprise when the next statement arrived
The cheque had been cashed on the funeral date.
She became hysterical when phoning her pal
Who advised her not to get in such a state.

'Trust your cunning Old Man to figure a way
To smuggle his dosh to a much hotter place.
Where all those fivers will curl up and burn,
Pity we won't see the shock on his face.

# 83. Oink, Oink, Get Out of My Way

These are tips for the aggressive
Who will drive however they like.
Use the horn to frighten the nervous,
Especially those clowns on a bike.
Approach roundabouts at top speed
And never let anyone in.
Keep the indicators turned off,
Maintain a self-satisfied grin.

On motorways ignore the rules
And go slow in the middle lane.
When leaving by the next exit,
Brake and swerve last minute again.
Speed limits are for the feeble,
So attack these cars from the rear,
Staying two feet from the bumper
Leave the driver shaking with fear.

If the front screen becomes icy
Scrape a small patch to peep through.
After a few miles it will melt,
Revealing a much clearer view.
Vehicles parked on the pavement
Should try not to leave a big gap
Or the car will become damaged
By the chair of a very old chap.

Bus lanes are not just for buses
But are also for special cars too.
No one must stop in box junctions
But of course that does not mean you.
When others are queuing in traffic
And the lane to the right is all clear.
Speed to the front without looking
Edge back in with a contemptuous sneer.

These pointers are for all geezers
Who live outside society's rules.
When they are out on the highway
Will gladly not tolerate 'fools'.
The question that they always ask
To friends at the end of the day.
How do road users pass their test
Driving in such a timorous way?

# 84. Retail Therapy

Do I have to go shopping again?
When I protest it's always in vain.
Half the time I am stood in the rain,
Do I have to go shopping again?

Should I manage a smile and pretend
To be part of the modern-day trend?
I am praying that soon it will end
And I won't have to smile and pretend.

Did I like the red and blue top
That we saw in the very first shop?
I do hope this nightmare will stop,
Yes, I loved the red and blue top.

Must we return to shop number one
To continue the shopping trip fun?
Back to where the trial had begun,
Let's not revisit shop number one.

Do you know what time we left the house?
I shouted at my shopping-mad spouse.
I had made up my mind not to grouse,
Oh, I wish I was back at the house.

Please can we stop a while for a drink,
We have both earned a break don't you think?
A refusal would make my heart sink,
I am sure it is time for a drink.

Do you think I have been a good sport
Carrying all this stuff you have bought?
It is very much more than I thought,
Oh, I wish he had taken up sport.

# 85. A Leisurely Drive

The Bottomley Family at house number five,
Organised a street party for those in the Drive.
There were forty-seven houses, most were detached,
Some looked Edwardian and a couple were thatched.
An invitation dropped on each neighbour's mat,
People who had not spoken soon started to chat.
'What is the occasion?' laughed Mrs McPhee,
The widow who lived in house twenty-three.
'It's so we can get to know one another,'
Replied Tracey Paine-Smith, an unmarried mother.

The day soon arrived and the marquee erected
Followed by 'Meet and Greet' which all were subjected.
'I am employed by the Crown' said Anthony Brand,
'I chop down some of the trees and clear all the land.'
'I am a police sergeant and my wife is a nurse.'
Answered the man who lived in the house that came first.
The couple from Germany from house number nine
Criticised all those who did not make it on time.
The last two to be questioned were Edith and Sid
Every one listened as they outlined what they did.

All the neighbours were ushered into the marquee,
A few rushed to the bar, but most wanted tea.
The sandwiches and rolls were hidden with a cloth
And the Scumbags tried to take the covering off.
Please leave the food alone shouted Dorothy Moore,
The carpenter's wife who was from house twenty-four.
We are having a quiz first and then we will eat
Announced the big mouth from the far end of the street.
The questions will be asked by Reverend Camper,
And the winners will get a very nice hamper.

The result was read out among boos and some moans,
The victorious team had been using their phones.
George Bottomley tried to say it was time to eat,
But his words got drowned out by a chorus of cheat.
It was not too long before the food was devoured,
In an atmosphere that had been poisoned and soured.
The captain of the quiz winners, a smug git, called Spence,
Raised a glass to the losers which made everyone tense.
It wasn't too long before the neighbours drifted away
They will never forget that memorable day.

# 86. The Man from the Pru

The insurance man knocked on the door,
'Who is it?' the parrot replied.
'It's the man from the Pru,'
Said the man from the Pru,
'Will you please let me inside?'

The insurance man knocked once again,
'Who is it?' the parrot replied.
'It's the man from the Pru'
Said the man from the Pru.
'I'm looking for Christopher Hyde.'

The insurance man battered with rage,
'Who is it?' the parrot replied.
'It's the man from the Pru'
Said the man from the Pru,
Then he fell on the floor where he died.

A policeman was soon on the scene.
'Who is it that's recently died?'
'It's the man from the Pru'
Said the mad cockatoo.
He's was looking for Christopher Hyde.

# 87. Short Back and Sides

Sweeney Todd, the local barber
Was joined by a cutter called Dave.
His eyes were bad, he had the shakes
No one went to him for a shave.
A new client called Danny O'Neil
Went and sat in the empty chair.
He soon felt that something was wrong
When he noticed the blood in his hair.

Dan started to shake and turn white,
His ear lobe was laid on the floor.
One customer brought up his lunch,
The rest made a dash for the door.
Sweeney picked up the severed piece
And wrapped it in a clean towel.
Dave was not aware what he'd done
Or able to see Danny's scowl.

David had forgotten his specs
Without them the room was a mist.
He had left them at the 'Red Lion'
The night he went out and got pissed.
Dan glanced in the mirror again
And saw all the gunge and the crap.
He tried to put on his glasses,
But they tumbled into his lap.

Dave said he had somewhere to go,
Refereeing a match down the Lane.
There wasn't time to go for his specs,
He'd make do without them again.
Dave sent a linesman to the stands
In his book he wrote the wrong names.
Each decision was a wild guess,
Yet this was one of Dave's better games.

# 88. Please Give Mummy a Break

Cameron, it is time for your bed,
Please do not forget to wash your face.
Make certain you brush and floss your teeth
And put all your toys back in their place.

Honey you have got five minutes left
Or I will unplug your PS Four.
I don't care if you've three men to kill,
It is not my fault you've lost your score.

Don't fib you could not have cleaned your teeth
Because your brush is completely dry.
Your flannel is like a summer's drought
I guess that's another white lie.

Teacher forgot to set your homework
You have had a lot more time to play.
No, you cannot stay up any longer
So please just pack all your stuff away.

Your controls appear to be in two,
Did they accidentally hit the wall?
My Angel you must take much more care,
No, you cannot have the day off school.

It doesn't matter if you're Captain Price
Or whoever else you'd like to be.
Close those big brown eyes and go to sleep,
Darling, do not make it hard for me.

Cameron, please give Mummy a break
And stop being a pain in the neck?
If you don't start to behave yourself,
I will end up a quivering wreck.

# 89. Heard It Through the Grapevine

Ade, you know the old girl at number two,
The one whose husband calls a silly moo.
If you get close to her you can smell drink
Her favourite tipple is whisky we think.
I know because Ruby told me so.

Ade, I have heard that her at number four
Has been divorced several times before.
I was told about her latest man today
And the reason why he keeps going away.
I know because Ruby told me so.

Ade, Lily's cousin they call Idle Jack
Swore at the boss and was given the sack.
He's gone away with young Margaret Queen,
They are heading up north to Gretna Green.
I know because Ruby told me so.

You remember the man at number five,
Well Ade, the rumour is he's been inside.
He is a small-time crook that's what they say,
Obviously for him crime does not pay.
I know because Ruby told me so.

Ade, have you wondered why Pat's always skint?
Her time in the bookies should give a hint.
She's been a punter since her early teens,
Bets on horses, greyhounds and fruit machines.
I know because Ruby told me so.

Ade, see those two, what an unfriendly pair,
You say hello and they'll just stand and stare.
She will never let him utter a word
Everyone says it's completely absurd.
I know because Ruby told me so.

Ade, someone's spreading gossip, it appears
Which has caused a lot of upset and tears.
Nobody is certain who it could be
At least we're sure it is not you or me.
Ruby will know and might tell us so.

# 90. Warts and All

Bernie made his dear wife promise him
That his eulogy would be the truth.
Tell the assembled what I was like
To this day from the time of my youth.

Sadly, on a bleak day in November
The Angels fetched Bernie away.
In her grief his spouse recalled the pledge
That she had made to her hubby that day.

Family, a neighbour and a friend
Gathered to celebrate Bernie's life.
Just as the deceased had requested,
The eulogy was read by his wife.

'My other half supported United
He had followed them since he was eight.
They wanted him to sign a contract
At least that's what he told his best mate.
Our honeymoon was spent in Clacton
Which was the last time we went away.
Although he would often remind me

That he took me to Ryde for the day.
His chair was in front of the tele,
In the exact place since we were wed.
The controller was clutched in his hand
That's how they found him when he was dead.
The fact is that Bernie was boring
He would send his work colleagues to sleep.
When it came to 'leaving' collections,
His arms were short and his pockets were deep.
My dear spouse was known as a tight arse,
He would always avoid buying a round.
But today the drinks are on Bernie,
After we've lowered him into the ground.
What more can I say about my man
And the characteristics we knew.
I vowed to him that I'd be honest
When describing his nature to you.

This ends the eulogy for Bernie,
He didn't try to be what he was not.
There was little charm or charisma
Because what you saw's what you got.'

Following the day of the committal
His epitaph was etched with great care.
'Here lies the body of Bernard Smith
Who was finally moved from his chair.'

# 91. Two Languages Collide

Granddad you are well sic.
*It's just a touch of gout.*
No fos I mean you're lit.
*I have put the fire out.*
Grumps I've got no cheddar.
*There's some cheese in the fridge.*
I need to buy some rides.
*Then go to London Bridge.*
You really are the goat.
*Then you must be the kid.*
OMG that's Gucci.
*Will you leave me for a quid?*
I'm gonna meet the squad.
*The flying or firing type?*
We meet to spill the tea.
*Make sure you take a wipe.*
I'm thirsty to hear the gab.
*Then don't upset your drink.*
Hearing you now I'm crine.
*I don't know what to think.*
You will pops just stay frosty.
*That's not easy when it's hot.*

It's all mad we can't even.
*You cannot even what?*
Hundo P, I've got to bounce.
*The trampoline's outside.*
Safe old, this is what happens,
*When two languages collide.*

# 92. Imagine No Line

Stood in a very long Post Office queue
Were Lilly, Gertrude, Barbara and Sue.
Barbara passed wind and blamed it on Lill,
The man stood in front begun to feel ill
And soon vacated the Post Office queue.

The next in line in the Post Office queue
Was a girl with several parcels to do.
Susan stepped forward to make a new friend
'I will call you if I'm at a loose end.'
The young lady left the Post Office queue.

There were now six at the front of the queue,
Lill lit a fag and blew smoke over Sue.
Two mothers said you are breaking the law
Which spurred Lilly on to exhale some more.
Coughing and choking the mums left the queue.

Gertrude's phone rang in the Post Office queue,
'Of course I'll give my bank details to you.'
A man snatched the mobile from Gerty's paw,
But couldn't hold on and it crashed to the floor.
Another dropped out of the Post Office queue.

Babs dentures fell on the ground by the queue,
She asked a young man if he had some glue.
'Please pick up my teeth and hand them to me.'
The youth threw up as he started to flee.
There was one less in the Post Office queue.

Two to remove from the Post Office queue
They shouted 'Do not worry we're going too.'
It took seconds before both disappeared
And in one hour the whole place had cleared.
Leaving the four at the front of the queue.

Milling around in the Post Office queue
Were Lilly, Gertrude, Barbara and Sue.
'Can I assist?' said cashier number two.
'No thank you luv we are just passing through.
We're off to disrupt another long queue.'

# 93. Judy Couldn't Come

There should have been twenty at the reunion,
But Judy couldn't come.
Samantha decided where each lady should sit,
This irritated some.
Doreen did not want to be seated next to Ann,
She had little choice.
Who would be voted 'Mutton dressed up as lamb'?
They thought it should be Joyce.
Mavis Lee got delayed and turned up very late,
'Sorry' was not enough.
Some talked about her when they knew she could not hear
And that was pretty tough.
Camille made an entrance and brought everyone a gift,
That's not what was agreed.
One of the party refused to accept their present,
There really was no need.
The assembled gathered into opposing groups,
It didn't pay to be slow.
Snatches of conversation could be overheard,
'I know, I know, I know.'
Each one glanced across the room and gave a knowing look,
It had got out of hand.

Luckily, the food arrived covered with tea towels,
The first one up was Jan.
Followed by all the factions in their dribs and drabs,
Good job looks can't kill.
Which of the angry women would pour out the drinks
And who would pay the bill?
Mildred Pike stood to speak to the reunion,
No one asked her to.
She said it was a pleasure to meet such great folk,
If only that were true.
The time had come to fetch the coats and say farewell,
Not too soon for most.
'What a great occasion we must all meet again,'
They all lied to the host.
There were hugs and kisses as the goodbyes were said,
The faces all looked glum.
The first to leave was Molly Stirritt who shouted,
'Pity Judy couldn't come.'

# 94. A Loyal Fan, Kipling Style

A loyal fan will never leave before the end
And at all times blame the referee for any loss.
He will trust the manager when all the others don't
But when he gets the sack, he will not give a toss.
A fan can wait one more season for promotion
And will never switch to support another team.
One day he is sure he'll see his side at Wembley,
Devoted supporters will always dream the dream.

In victory he shouldn't make gloating his mantra,
When he loses be prepared to take it on the chin.
Should it go quiet in the away end let them know
And remind them not to sing only when they win.
If there's a need to shout don't make the ref the aim,
He's probably left his spectacles in the car.
Do not advise the lineman where to stick his flag
Because that would be going quite a bit too far.

Before a game chat with the away supporters,
Praise their sides most recent entertaining displays.
When there have been a run of defeats, don't forget to—
Have faith that your team will get back to winning ways.
While at work after the team have just lost a match
Smile at all your colleagues and let them have their fun.
Tell them it's not the score that counts but being there
And if you can do this, you'll be a fan, my son.

# 95. Trooper Tommy Trotter

Trooper Trotter sat astride his mount
At the start of another parade.
He'd never ridden this horse before
Or witnessed a staff sergeant's tirade.
The soldier sat upright in the saddle,
Tightly gripping his sword with much fear.
His arm suddenly jolted forward
As he severed his trusty steed's ear.
The nag made a dash for the exit,
His rider holding on for dear life.
He prayed like you do in a crisis,
Thinking he'd never get home to his wife.

The horse swerved left into the traffic
And made its' way towards Tower Hill.
The petrified man held on tightly,
Bringing to bear his limited skill.
The charger pulled up by the Tower,
Flinging the guardsman on to the ground.

Then it headed back to the barracks
Where the dishevelled equine was found.
Meanwhile the bruised and battered trooper
Was whisked off in a hurry to Barts.
He needed his injuries treated
And have X-rays to some of his parts.

As Tommy Trotter lay in his bed,
Wondering what'd become of his horse.
Hopefully he was back in his box
And his ear had been stitched back of course.
The staff sergeant marched into the ward
Spouting a string of equine based puns.
He was there to take back the sabre,
Now Tom will have to make do with guns.
Next time the trooper went to the stalls,
He had to groom the mount with one ear.
The charger turned to show his sharp teeth
Kicking out when he smelt Tommy's fear.

# 96. Tunnel Vision

Eddie became claustrophobic
In the year Nineteen Seventy-Four.
His tube train broke down in a tunnel,
He was there for an hour or more.
Ed alighted at the next station
Where his anxiety started to fall.
He'd travelled that line for a decade
Without hitting the metaphorical wall.

It was a long walk to his office
And he'd never before turned up late.
How would he get home that evening
And why had Eddie suffered this fate?
When the poor man reached his workplace,
Negative thoughts continued to drift.
His panic returned very quickly
Because he had to enter the lift.

This day saw the start of Ed's nightmare,
It was something he could not explain.
The sheer panic and palpitations
Every time he got on a train.
All his tube journeys had to be planned
And his deep breathing had to be right.
Although life had become quite a challenge
At the end of the tunnel was light.

# 97. What a Pantomime

Jack, what's with those magic beans?
You've fallen for a scam it seems.
Why did you swap your Mother's cow?
I bet you feel quite silly now.
Cinderella please get real
And even with the best of will.
A mouse can't become a horse
Which means you're staying home of course.

Whittington make up your mind,
You seem to be the turning kind.
Dick, you're so easily led
With sounds of bells inside your head.
You do not fly—Peter Pan,
Despite the fact you think you can.
Go on dreaming if you must,
But clear up all that fairy dust.

Sneezy you should blow your nose
And Bashful buy some raunchy clothes.
Dopey start to use your loaf,
Doc learn the Hippocratic oath.
Happy your smile is cringing,
Grumpy stop the constant whingeing.
And Sleepy try to stay awake,
Snow White wise up for goodness sake.

# 98. A Day in the Life of a Backbencher

Nigel Ponsonby-Smythe gets up early
And takes Winston, his bulldog, for a walk.
He worries about meeting constituents,
In case he is forced to smile, stop and talk.
When his dog starts to pull hard to the left
It is a sign to go back to the house.
There he must answer a tricky question,
Tabled by his Right Honourable Spouse.

'What cereal do you want for breakfast?'
Lady Jacqueline asks every day.
'Please refer to my previous answer.'
So he is given cornflakes on a tray.
Once the Member for Poshside has finished,
He chooses one of his blue ties to wear.
He sits on a Select Committee,
This week it is his turn to chair.

The first task is to choose the lunch menus
And pick curtains for the Members club room.
Moving on to approve all expense claims
Which will mean the cleaner gets a new broom.
At noon the Committee retire to eat,
Cabinet pudding is the treat of the day.
Afternoon is constituency business
When the hoi polloi can all have their say.

Lady Jacqueline is sometimes annoyed
Because quite often he's late for his tea.
'You pass more of your time with your colleagues
Than you'd ever think of spending with me.
Tell me Nigel what is my best feature,
You used to say it was my lovely smile?
I can't believe you said the eyes have it,
You have certainly lost none of your style.'

Most evenings for Sir Nigel are hectic
With appointments to appear on T.V.
His opinions are sought on many issues
And there is never a moment that's free.
'Let me be clear' he'd say in confusion
While not answering the question that's posed.
'I've nothing further to add at this time,
So I am afraid this matter is closed.'

He promised he would be home by midnight,
But was delayed and turned up a bit late.
The upper house was locked and in darkness
And the Right Honourable Spouse made him wait.
Once he gained entry into the lobby,
He was told 'You kip on the sofa bed.'
Where he dreamt of becoming a statesman
Until he was disturbed by Winston's cold head

# 99. Illegitime Nil Carborundum

When most of the year of Seventy-Nine
Went back to their old school next to the Tyne.
It was a night when the braggers did brag
And the old head boy turned up wearing drag.
The smartest kid who was top of the class
Fell on his back as he slipped on the grass.
Billy, the bullshitting fool, drew a crowd,
Relating his exploits overly loud.
Jan, the prettiest girl back in the day
Looked very mumsy, her hair had turned grey.
The lad they thought wasn't supposed to be bright,
Drove a Ferrari and talked through the night.
The nasty school bully shook like a leaf,
He was unsure if he'd get any grief.
It didn't take long for his fate to be sealed,
His suit got all muddy out on the field.
The headmaster was unable to come,
All was explained in a note from his mum.
The evening's surprise was when in walked Gerd
Because they thought he was still doing bird.
Wallets and purses were hidden away
He wasn't jailed for theft, but for causing affray.

Diane was the last to come through the door,
Everyone noticed the dress that she wore.
Barbara Lee had the same one in green,
They both kept apart so they wouldn't be seen.
No one had seen 'Casanova' about,
His partner would not trust him to be out.
Once considered 'Lower Heights' alpha male,
Muscles McKenzie was now looking frail.
He could not remove the top off his beer,
It was lucky 'Weedy' Johnson was near.
The evening progressed, the decibels rose,
At last the proceedings came to a close.
'Remember the school motto' said the class clown
'Don't let the bastards grind anyone down.'

# 100. Remember the Days of the Lockdown

Remember the days of the lockdown
When all the hairdressers were shut.
Many of us relied on our spouses
To get our unruly locks cut.
Remember the queues at the checkout
With toilet rolls stacked to the top.
The hoarders that kept the stores empty,
Whenever they swooped on a shop.
Remember the curve that we flattened
And the Thursdays when we all clapped.
The advisor who drove up to Durham,
And very nearly got himself sacked.
Remember the beaches in Bournemouth,
Tons of litter left on the sand.
All the masks that covered our faces
And how some things got out of hand.
Remember the distancing mantra,
When we all kept two metres apart.
Health Secretary, Matthew Hancock
Showing one more Government chart.
Remember the empty stadiums

And the 'R' rate that had to be low.
The front-line workers and the teachers
Who put on a lifesaving show.
Remember we got vaccinations,
The eighties were given theirs first.
The hope was that things would get better,
For a time they seemed to get worse.
Remember when the schools reopened
And most of the children were glad.
Not having to think about Brexit,
The test and trace that drove us all mad.
Remember Professor Jon Van-Tam
And the analogies that he used.
New words like furlough and variant,
Left some of us completely confused.
Remember those who worked from home
Without ever seeing their boss.
Those daily reported statistics
Showing every heart-breaking loss.
Remember when we forgot about COVID
And started to mix once again.
The parties that reportedly happened
Bringing all that political pain.